C000304145

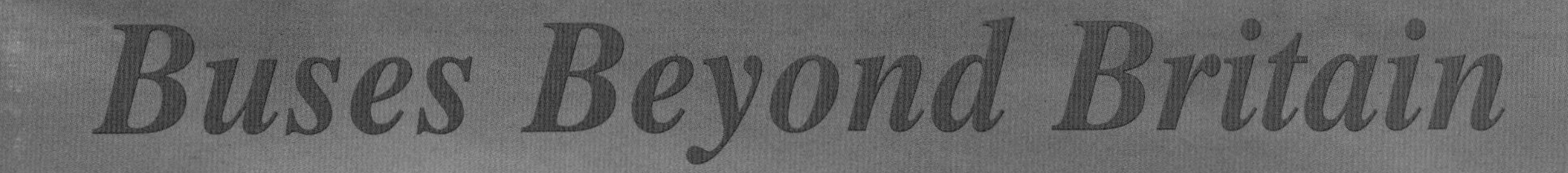

Buses Beyond Britain

Paul Haywood

Venture *publications*

ISBN 1 905304 08 0

Front cover: Australian Pacific Tours **103**, an ex-West Riding Automobile Services (672) Alexander-bodied Daimler Fleetline, was working as a Melbourne City Explorer bus when seen outside Flinders Street station in February 1993. The author probably rode on this bus in its home territory back in the 1970s.

Rear cover: Greyhound of Canada **689**, an MCI MC-9 of 1982, had just delivered a group of Japanese tourists to Banff to join VIArail's "The Canadian" for a spectacular trip through the Rockies to Kamploops and Vancouver in September 1989.

Title page: ERF (now owned by MAN) was never a major player in the UK bus industry, but did develop a substantial market for buses, as well as the more usual trucks, in South Africa. This example has a Coach Tech body and belongs to tour operator Stevens. It was at Mossel Bay, Cape Province, in November 1998.

Right: Huge housing and commercial developments have taken place in all parts of the Hong Kong New Territories over the past 20 years. In April 1989, these high-rise flats were being built above the Kowloon Canton Railway bus/light rail depot in Tuen Mun - a useful source of income where land is at a premium. Typical bamboo scaffolding acts as a dramatic backdrop to KCR **122**, an MCW Metrobus.

>> ***Opposite page:*** Yellowstone Park **517**, an MCI type MC-5B, waits to connect with the daily Seattle to Chicago Greyhound bus service at Livingston, Montana, in September 1982. Until ten years earlier, park buses would also have met the daily Northern Pacific "North Coast Limited" train to transfer visitors to Yellowstone's famous Old Faithful Geyser and Lodge Hotel.

OLD FAITHFUL
517
517
YELLOWSTONE
YELLOWSTONE PARK
TWA
787
517
35

Dedication

To my late wife Sue, for her patience, tolerance and acceptance of my love for road and rail transport.
To my new wife Yvonne, for bravely taking me on *in spite* of my love for road and rail transport.

INTRODUCTION

Welcome to "Buses Beyond Britain". Why "Beyond Britain"? Well, one reason was the imbalance in favour of UK titles in the portfolios of many British bus book publishers. Would train or tram publishers have such a narrow perspective?

Thankfully, John Banks of Venture Publications was prepared to accept my suggestion for this book, and I am both grateful and proud to be able to present this snapshot (literally and metaphorically) of buses in various parts of the world captured on film by me over the past 34 years.

In the early 1970s I started to venture overseas, camera at the ready, and became reacquainted with my first love, the tram. In a book about buses, I won't dwell on the trams too much (they may well be the subject of a companion volume), but it is with them that "*Buses* Beyond Britain" starts to take shape.

Over 30 years ago my knowledge of buses beyond Britain was virtually nil, although there were some familiar names. Leyland and AEC still had a strong presence in some parts of Europe at that time, but DAF and MAN meant little, and surely Mercedes, Volvo, Renault and Fiat were cars not buses? Those "foreign" dual-entrance, underfloor-engined single-deckers held little attraction for me, with their quiet engines, smooth suspension and automatic transmission. They bore no relation to the throaty, gear-crunching British buses I once knew and loved.

European holidays at that time were mainly tram-orientated (wife *usually* permitting, but with caveats about being fed regularly, or having a few days by a poolside) and I barely noticed, let alone photographed, the buses I saw passing in the streets. Because of the anti-tram feelings in Britain at that time, I took a very biased stance in their favour, and thought that buses competed with the tram, so it would surely be treachery to take an interest in them.

And so things remained until the 1980s when, through my job, I was lucky enough to have the opportunity to travel further afield, and personal finance allowed more adventurous holidays. As there often weren't many or any trams in some locations, I started to take note of the local buses whenever the opportunity arose. Although carrying a 35mm SLR camera on business was not an easy thing to do when you were expected to take only a briefcase to a meeting, I tried to keep it handy whenever possible. I also tried to create time between or after meetings, or on weekends between flights, when I would venture forth into the streets for brief but valuable hours.

Unfortunately, there were many missed opportunities either because my camera was back at the hotel, or it would have seemed rude, strange or time-wasting if I had asked my agent to stop the car so I could photograph a bus. The cliché of the "eccentric Englishman" would have been reinforced. If only I had had the courage to shout "stop the car!"

The world wide bus industry has seen countless buy-outs, take-overs, closures and mergers. What may have been a well-established chassis or body builder in one country could now be part of another group based thousands of miles away. It's likely that within the time taken to prepare this book there have been more changes, so some of my captions may be out of date or inaccurate. The one certainty is that a lot has happened to the bus industry in the three decades covered by this book. Buses, like many things today, are now truly international.

Deregulation and privatisation, both in the UK and elsewhere was, I believe, in the early years a disaster. It lowered standards, raised fares and forced many bus passengers away from public transport altogether. Some countries made the transition from public to private better than others. However, many former Communist countries are now struggling to cope with the massive change from high levels of patronage (albeit with heavily subsidised fares) to unregulated, almost pirate, operations run for a quick profit. The USA went down this road in the 1920s and 30s and they are still living with the public transport consequences.

Thankfully, there is renewed optimism in the bus industry, and genuine efforts are being made by operators and manufacturers to improve the quality of service and vehicles to help stem the flow away from bus usage.

So, over the past thirty-odd years I have accumulated a collection of photographs of Buses Beyond Britain. I don't claim to be a good photographer, and my range of locations and vehicles in the thirty-plus countries represented in this book may not be as comprehensive as some may wish. However, in deference to my British readers, and to reflect my own interest, the selection includes a proportion of views of vehicles with a British theme, be they former British-operated, British-built or British-influenced. Consequently, I have given extra coverage to those vehicles and locations I believe have greater interest to a British reader, such as Hong Kong, Malta, and Ireland. Additionally, I have emphasised vehicles that reflect my personal interest, like the US Park buses and the Burma rebuilds.

Researching for this book has not been easy. I never kept a notebook of exact locations and dates, relying instead on memory or diaries. Internet enquiries about vehicle origin to bus enthusiasts in various countries have often been unsuccessful, as the photographs were probably taken too many years ago for the comparatively young enthusiasts using this mode of communication. However, I am grateful to those who were able to give me some information, and am pleased to acknowledge them accordingly. I now wish I had taken more notice of those makers' badges and operators details. Those photographs for which I could find little or no information of vehicle builder or operator have been kept in with the basic information in the hope that the picture speaks louder than the words. Perhaps, one day, there will be the equivalent of the PSV Circle in every country in the world!

I now find myself having come full circle. "Buses Beyond Britain" have kept my interest alive when buses in Britain seemed so mundane. I never thought that, back in the dark days of the 1970s, I would see trams back in the streets of Britain, and buses would be interesting again.

For simplicity, I have presented the photographs alphabetically by country. Students of politics and geography will note that I prefer to list Myanmar as the more familiar Burma; I have kept Hong Kong as a separate country for no other reason than their fleets are so specific and unique to their territory. So, on page six we start in Australia and on page 80 we finish in the USA.

I hope you enjoy the trip.

I would like to thank the following people and organisations for helping me to solve some the puzzles about vehicle details and origins: Maurice Bateman, Paul Bateson, Mike Butler, Won-Ho Choi, David Corke, Simon Garden, Mark Harrington, "Herman", John Hinson, "The Inspector", Dave Reesby. Essential information was gleaned from *Malta Bus Album* (Venture Publications), *The Malta Bus Handbook* (British Bus Publishing) and *The Malta Buses* (Bonnici/Cassar, Malta). My apologies for any omissions made in error rather than intent.

Finally, I should like to thank Mary and Dave Shaw for reading the proofs and John Banks for production and editorial help.

Paul Haywood
North Yorkshire
June 2005

50
MORTLAKE
VINTAGE VEHICLE
1615
Albion
003

AUSTRALIA

← Sydney **1615**, a magnificent Albion CX19 with Waddington body of 1939, was saved for posterity and preserved at the Loftus Transport Museum when seen in October 1982. It is now part of Sydney's Tempe Bus Museum collection.

↑ Ansett Roadways originally operated this International KB-6. Unfortunately, enquiries about body manufacturer and year into service have proved fruitless. In February 1993 it was running local tours for Sentimental Journeys in the Adelaide area and is seen at the nearby coastal resort of Glenelg.

AUSTRALIA

The Adelaide O-Bahn (guided busway) opened in 1986 and at twelve kilometres long is still claimed to be the world's longest and fastest (perhaps because there are only two intermediate stations on the guided section). Mercedes-Benz supplied both articulated and non-articulated 0305s fitted with guide-wheels especially for the "Busway" route. These views were taken in February, 1993. ↑ Articulated **1591** arrives at one of the two intermediate stations. Note, in the left-hand lane, the 100 km/h speed limit sign, and the yellow line to help drivers aim for the guided section. ➔ O-Bahn non-articulated **1540** is seen approaching the Tea Tree Plaza terminus.

SPECIAL
1540

AUSTRIA

↑ The Wien Lokalbahn operates an interurban light rail route from Vienna to the spa town of Baden. Lokalbahn **48**, a smart MAN/Graf & Stift, meets the tram at Baden terminus in October 1988.

BELGIUM

➔ Belgium was famous for its nationwide interurban and rural public transport system commonly known as the Vicinal (SNCV/NMVB), with its huge network of steam, petrol, diesel and electric trams and light railways. Most of the routes were converted to bus operation in the 1950s and 1960s. At Maurage in 1983 is tram **9140** having just arrived on the circuitous 110 minute run from Charleroi (as route 80) while DAF/Van Hool **2070** prepares to take connecting passengers onward to Mons. Until 1962, the tram would have operated throughout.

17 MONS HAVRE
MAURAGE
31
AUTOBUS
2070
VANHOOL
1217P

BURMA

↑ During World War Two, many thousands of Canadian-built, right-hand drive Chevrolet and Ford lorries were built for British, Commonwealth and Allied use in most areas of conflict. After the war against the Japanese in South East Asia, many of these Canadian Military Pattern (CMP) trucks were rebuilt as buses to a US style with standee windows. Because of its British colonial history, Burma had left-hand rule of the road (with right-hand drive), as do the adjacent countries of India, Malaysia and Thailand, so these CMPs were well suited. Perversely, even though many vehicle imports were right-hand drive from Japan and India, Burma converted to right-hand rule of the road in 1970. On a humid Rangoon morning in 1986, examples of an original CMP Ford lorry and a bus rebuild make an interesting comparison.

→ In the Rangoon evening rush hour in June 1987, passengers on this CMP bus are importuned by a passing beggar boy practising his unfortunate trade. The Cargo lorry bus behind needs some good old-fashioned elbow grease to get it restarted.

BURMA

↑ If buses could talk, what tales they could tell. This wonderful line-up of CMP buses was seen in Mandalay in October 1982. Identification of origin is now virtually impossible as these vehicles will have been cannibalised and rebuilt many times since the war by the ever-resourceful but cash-poor Burmese operators. ↗ "Standing room only". → At the Shwe Tha Lyaung shrine to the image of the reclining Buddha near Pegu, this suitably exotic normal-control Chevrolet lorry bus has just pulled in to exchange passengers in July 1986. The colourful cover would be a vital shield against either the blazing sun or monsoon rain.

THE SHWE THA LYAUNG IMAGE
LAVATORY

BURMA

↑ In Rangoon in June 1987 an unexpected sight was this example of a small batch of newly imported Paris Saviem SC10s built in 1974, still bearing RATP colours and fleet number **6658**. The popularity of this bus is evident by the crush load. The CMP bus behind had an official maximum load of 30 passengers - rarely observed - so this ex-Paris bus must have seemed massive. Note the lighting poles that had been used to carry tram wires until the Japanese invasion in 1943, and the beautiful Sule Pagoda that dominates the background.

CANADA

→ Toronto Transit Commission **3950** represents the GM "New Look" style which became very popular throughout North America in the 1970s. This example is seen at the then northern-most subway station of York Mills in October 1973.

VICTORIA PK.
3950

CHINA

➔ Kowloon Motor Bus runs a joint venture operation in Dalian in north-east China. These somewhat angular former KMB Baco-bodied Fleetlines **13**, **19** and **16**, as well as ex-London DMS **03**, are allocated to Dalian route 401, and are seen during off-peak layover in September 2000.

CZECH REPUBLIC

➔ The Czech bus maker Karosa has, since privatisation in 1993, developed a range of vehicles in collaboration with Renault and Ikarus (now Irisbus). These two C954E intercity coaches operated by CSAD Liberec are seen in their home town in February 2004, in seasonal weather.

Linka 540001
1L3 9529
Liberec
Praha
ČSAD Liberec, a.s.
1L4 2925

DENMARK

← Because of its reliability and low height, the Bristol Lodekka found a ready market in many parts of the world for promotional and tourist purposes. By June 2000, this former Southern Vectis example (546), was relegated to the mundane role of a static advertising hoarding in Copenhagen.

FINLAND

→ The Finnish national bus system is a vast consortium of operators covering even the most remote communities in this sparsely populated country. Oy Matkahuolto operates all the nation's coach terminals, offering through ticketing, reservations, refreshment facilities and an important baggage and parcels service. These Scania Kutters were working for Satakunnan Liikenne Oy (left) and Valtaliikenne Ky (right) when seen at Rauma bus station and parcels office in July 1988.

→ → Another Bristol Lodekka, this time ex-Wilts and Dorset (688) operating for Top Deck Travel. Named "Leylandi", it is seen outside Senate Square Cathedral, Helsinki, in July 1988. Top Deck Travel has always been a keen user of Lodekkas and their "backpacker" tour buses have been seen in many countries throughout the world.

PORI
RAUMA
RAUMA-EURAJOKI
LAUTTAKYLÄ
SCANIA
TOB-135
TOT-820

Leyland
top deck travel

GERMANY

➔ In the early days of German reunification in October 1990, major efforts were made to help former East German citizens become more financially aware. To assist this, the Bonn government arranged for temporary banks to be set-up in former East German locations. This Bonn-registered Mercedes Benz 0305 was acting in a mobile role for the Berliner Bank, when seen in Potsdam only days after the two countries formally became one again. ➔ On the same day, BVG (West Berlin) **3205**, a MAN SD79/Waggon Union built in 1979, is arriving in Potsdam on a popular "over the wall" Sunday sightseeing service from the Wansee S-Bahn station. Behind is a Potsdam Ikarus 280 of 1975 - a workhorse of the final days of East European Communism.

H
BUS
99E
Potsdam
Bassinplatz
GRAWERT
WAGGON UNION
B-V 3205
3205

GERMANY

← How are the mighty fallen! London Routemaster RM2136 seems doomed to spend its last years as a children's playroom at this McDonald's autobahn restaurant south of Munich. Perhaps RM stands for Ronald McDonald after all? The photograph was taken in April 2001.

→ London Transport Leyland RTW335 is seen at the Hannover Expo park acting as a static weight demonstrator for Hywema vehicle lifts in April 1985. Luckily, this bus is now safely back in the UK for restoration and preservation.

Kilburn Marble Arch
Oxford Circus
Piccadilly Circus
266
EDGWARE STATION
HYWEMA
D 5650 SOLINGEN
SICHER
42
mtr.
NIMBUS
HYWEMA

GREECE

↑ In 1983 these ECW bodied Leyland Olympians appeared on the streets of Athens for an airport express service. They are seen at the old airport's West Terminal in January 1990. Even Athens winters are cold enough to require some rudimentary radiator insulation!

HONG KONG

→ Probably the only place in the world (outside museums and Fleetwood on the UK's Blackpool system) where both double-deck trams and buses can still be seen sharing the same road space is on Hong Kong Island. The front seat of the top deck of a tram is the best place to witness the endless cavalcade of buses and trams. Here we see Kowloon Motor Bus **3AD168** a Dennis Dragon with Duple Metsec body in September 2000. The buses on the left represent the New World First Bus group which, together with Citybus, took over the routes of China Motor Bus on the expiry of its franchise in 1998.

61
Est. 1904
兒童
傷風素
Shaukeiwan
筲箕灣
Children's
COLTALIN
61
127
SHUN LEE
619
HT475

HONG KONG

↑ On a wet April morning in 1989 we see China Motor Bus **LV135** and **LV101**, 1981 Leyland Victory 2s with Alexander bodywork, at the Central Ferry bus station. This style of bus dominated the streets of Hong Kong and Kowloon in the 1980s. The Victory 2 was basically a Guy with a Leyland badge and represented some of the last output of the famous Wolverhampton factory. → Citybus **D19**, a former London DMS-class Daimler Fleetline was offering a free shuttle to take tourists from the Star Ferry Terminal to the Peak Tram lower station in April 1989.

STAR FERRY
天星碼頭
LOWER TERMINAL
PEAK TRAM
Citybus
城巴
D19
山頂纜車
FREE SHUTTLE SERVICE 免費穿梭巴士
CP 2847
PEAK TRAM
FREE SHUTTLE BUS
免費接駁巴士
STAR FERRY
M.T.R. CENTRAL
LOWER TERMINAL

HONG KONG

↑ The Tuen Mun light rail system serves a large and developing region in the New Territories. Feeding into it is Kowloon Motor Bus **G261**, a 1980 Leyland Victory 2 with Alexander bodywork, seen passing a light rail vehicle on Castle Peak Road, Yuen Long in January 1995. → China Motor Bus **XF58** is an ex-London Daimler Fleetline (DMS479) with Park Royal body and **LV111** a 1981 Leyland Victory 2 with Alexander body, seen in February 1991. The once familiar blue and cream CMB buses are now history, the operator having lost the franchise in 1998.

11
JARDINE'S LOOKOUT 渣甸山
XF58
CJ 7614
CAUSEWAY BAY
銅鑼灣
72
LV111
CN9574
CMB

HONG KONG

🡅 Hong Kong operators have been faithful to the concept of the double-decker for many years, encouraging innovation and good design. Citybus **619** is a Volvo Olympian with Plaxton body, and Kowloon Motor Bus **ATS34** a Dennis Trident with bodywork by Duple Metsec. They are seen at the Tin Shui Wai bus/light rail interchange in the New Territories in September 2000.

HUNGARY

➔ British double-deckers can be found in many parts of the world and, if painted red, often masquerade as London buses. This ex-East Kent Park Royal-bodied AEC Regent V (MFN 950F) of 1967 had London Transport markings and fleet number **RM7950**, and was in use as a mobile sales stand at the Budapest Exhibition Park in 1993.

THERMO
LTD
ENERGETIKAI BEMUTATÓ
PADLÓFŰTÉS - NAPENERGIA
SZÁMÍTÓGÉPES FŰTÉSTERVEZÉS SZERELVÉNYÁRUSÍTÁS
THERMO
Vaillant

HUNGARY

← London Transport Routemaster **RM2205** stands proudly in the streets of Budapest in April 1993, but sadly the only boarders will be refreshment seekers in this unusual café.

IRISH REPUBLIC

→ Buses in the Irish Republic always had a reputation for being slightly different to British eyes, and they richly deserve a place in the "Beyond Britain" category. Here is an example of the once ubiquitous Coras Iompair Éireann (CIE) bodied Leyland Titan. **R827** is an OPD2/10 built in 1958 to an all-Leyland style dating from 10 years earlier. In October 2001 it was preserved at a privately run agricultural and transport museum at Ballinhassig near Cork, but has since moved to the nearby Kells Transport Museum.

HALFWAY
USE
YR
SAUCE
AERPHORT
USE
SALAD CREAM
GOLDEN AMBER
CYI 629

IRISH REPUBLIC

🡩 This July 1984 Conyngham Road, Dublin, depot line-up shows, from left to right, CIE Leyland Atlantean/CIE/Metal Sections **D282** of 1969, Atlantean/Van Hool **D834** of 1977, unidentified Bombardier of 1981-3, Atlantean/CIE/Metal Sections **D350** of 1970 and Atlantean/Van Hool **D790** of 1976. Thankfully, the khaki livery was on borrowed time. ➔ Because of the unreliability of the early Atlanteans, CIE's long-lasting love for Leyland products evaporated in the late 1970s when they opted for a rather unusual vehicle from the Canadian company Bombardier to a German (FFG) design. Mostly fitted with GM engines, they were home-built in Shannon. In 1987 the state-run CIE split its bus and rail empire into Bus Éireann, Dublin Bus and Iarnrod Éireann. Now sporting the Dublin Bus logo, Bombardier **KD321** of 1983 waits to take up Rail Link duties at Heuston station in September 1990.

City Centre An Lar
They've saved the best trip for last.
But this time they may have gone too far.
PAY AS YOU ENTER
DUBLIN BUS
GSI 321
KD321

IRISH REPUBLIC

🡑 Soon after completion of some 366 double-deckers in 1983, Bombardier lost control of the Shannon factory to GAC who continued to build single-deckers to a similar format for CIE's city, rural and coach operations. Bus Éireann GAC rural buses **KR92/1** of 1985 are seen outside Sligo railway station in September 1990.

ISRAEL

➔ The DAN Company operate city buses in Tel Aviv, and in 1990 these examples were typical of their fleet. **3533** is a MAN SL200 of 1983 with Ha'argas bodywork and **3076** is a MAN SL200 of 1977 with a Merkavim body.

3 5
35
MAN
50·603·83
3076
M·A·N
336·737

ISRAEL

↑ Egged, the massive Israeli bus co-operative, operates throughout the country. **20602** is an example of a Mercedes-Benz 0303 with Merkavim dual-purpose body built in 1984. It was photographed between runs at Tel Aviv bus station in January 1990.

ITALY

→ Orange-liveried Fiat buses epitomised the Italian scene for many years, and these Menarini Fiat 421ALs were typical. ATC (Bologna) **4056** was at the city's railway station operating a connecting service direct to the Exhibition Centre in November 1988.

B
entrata
uscita
entrata
Atc
4056 entrata
4056

KUWAIT

↑ In 1996 Kuwait was still struggling to recover from the first Gulf War, a consequence of which was that a large proportion of the population left the country - some never to return. Demand for public transport therefore reduced considerably, but this pair of Ikarus 263s (**5344** and **5358**) gamely continued service.

MALAYSIA

→ British business in Malaysia took a severe setback in the 1980s under the Malaysian government's "Buy British Last" policy. Since then, attitudes have mellowed and these Optare Metrorider MR17s, locally built under licence by DRB-Hicom, and operated by Intrakota for services in the Klang Valley area, made a familiar sight when seen at Sea Park terminus in Petaling Jaya in September 1995.

38 SEA PARK
JLN 21/1 P.JAYA
INTRAKOTA
WDP 4061
KOTA

MALTA

The island has long been famous for its fascinating array of British chassis with local bodies, many of a considerable age and complex lineage - some civil, some military. All these views were taken in the summer of 1985 at the Mecca for bus enthusiasts - Valletta bus station. Since then, there has been a change of livery from green and white to yellow with orange and white, and all the buses were reregistered in 1995. ↑ **Y-0563** is a Ford Thames with Sammut body; rather more familiar to UK readers is **Y-0345**, an AEC Reliance with Willowbrook body (ex-Cynon Valley 4). Note the painted-out sun roof windows, a necessity in Malta's climate. ➔ **Y-0310** is a Bedford OB with Brincat bodywork and simple but practical air-cooling for both engine and driver.

18
Y-0310
Coca-Cola

MALTA

↑ **Y-0735** is an ex-Pulfrey, of Great Gonerby, Bedford YRQ fitted with Duple Dominant coachwork, and was one of a large intake of second-hand British buses imported in the early 1980s to replace older vehicles. **Y-0704** is a Brincat-bodied Austin K4, and **Y-0529** is a British Dodge with Aquilina bodywork.
→ **Y-0458** is a Mallia bodied US-style Dodge. Its smart and simple design seemed to epitomise the classic look of an early postwar normal control bus, so typical of the period.

4
Y-0458

MALTA

↑ **Y-0763** will be recognised by many British readers as ex-London Transport SMS34, an AEC Swift with Marshall bodywork. → These are magnificent examples of the "dodgem-car", or "jukebox", styling that typified the "Maltese look". **Y-0361** is a Sammut-bodied Bedford QLD and **Y-0322** is a Barbara-bodied Bedford SB.

65
47
Y-0361
Y-0322

MEXICO

↑ An interesting comparison of US school bus styles (on vehicles probably built in Mexico) is seen in Cuidad Juarez with a Chevrolet overtaking an International, both in use on stage-carriage services in October 2000. → This example of a US-style (and probable origin) school bus is seen in the early morning sun preparing to transport hotel guests to one of the viewing points of the Copper Canyon. The vehicle's rugged build and austere internal fittings guaranteed a bumpy ride for passengers on the potholed dirt roads. The photograph was taken at Cerocahui, Sierra Madre, October 2000.

TURISMO
HOTEL MISION

MEXICO

🡅 This DINA with Marco Polo Viaggio body, operated by Americanos (a subsidiary of the US Greyhound Company), was photographed pulling into a rest stop at El Sueco en route to Chihuahua in October 2000.

NETHERLANDS

➔ GVU (Utrecht) **905** is a 24-metre long double-articulated Van Hool AGG300, seen standing at the city's Centraal rail/bus interchange in June 2004. They were designed to operate a specially authorised route between there and the University. The requirements for large turning circles and avoidance of the need to reverse scarcely need stressing.

12 Centraal Station
905
GVU
ZZ-63-89

NEW ZEALAND

↑ Auckland's Yellow Bus Company **1501** is a Mercedes 0305 with a body by NZ Motor Bodies to the familiar German VoV specification built in 1977. It was photographed off-duty at the city's main railway station in February 1993. → The local bus meets the daily train from Auckland at Rotorua's utilitarian railway station in February 1993. Reesby **7** is a MAN SL202 with a Coachwork International (NZ) body. It was supplied new to New Plymouth City Council in 1986, then passing to Goldstar Bus Lines on privatisation in 1991, until that company failed later the same year, when it was bought by Reesby. Since this scene was photographed, the bus has moved on to Leopard Coachlines in Christchurch.

08
NGONGOTAHA KOUTU
REESBYS
M·A·N
NH2687
InterCity

NEW ZEALAND

↑ There can't be many places outside Britain where a London Routemaster could seem so "at home"; in fact one has to look a second time to realise that this is not a scene in Tottenham Court Road. **RM1670** was on city tour duties on Quay Street, Auckland, in February 1993. ➔ The Museum of Transport and Technology in Auckland contains a fascinating collection of buses and trolleybuses, as well as a working tramway. Interesting exhibits photographed in February 1993 were 1953 vintage Saunders-Roe-bodied Leyland Royal Tiger (**464**) and Daimler Freeline (**201**).

PT CHEVALIER
5
464 AUCKLAND REGIONAL AUTHORITY
464
EZ 2641
SYMONDS ST
10E
ROUTE
201
EZ 2454

POLAND

🡩 The articulated Ikarus 280s were produced in vast numbers and gave service in most Eastern European countries in the final years of Communism. Warsaw **3014** stands at Wilanow terminus in September 1991. ➔ A novel use was found for this severed rear end of a Warsaw Ikarus bus to create a cosy and well-maintained staff rest room at Esperanto terminus. The rear of complete **2587** makes an interesting contrast in September 1991. Was fleet number **007** genuine, or an ironic dig at the hard-liners of Poland's recently deposed political regime?

111
2587
WAB
328P
007

PORTUGAL

↑ These Lisbon left-hand-drive AEC Regent IIIs and Vs with Weymann half-cab bodies always make a British viewer look twice. Busy in the evening rush hour, they jockey for position as the tram calmly goes about its business at Praca do Comercio in August 1981. ➔ Because the Lisbon tramway and bus system was registered in London and operated under a concession until 1973, there was a considerable British influence on the vehicles purchased. Among the last of these was a 1967 batch of Daimler Fleetlines, fitted with CCFL (Companhia Carris de Ferro de Lisboa) bodywork. Number **826** makes a strange contrast of scale with tram **613** at Martim Moniz in August 1981.

S. TOME
12
613
Tudor
MOSCAVIDE
8

SAUDI ARABIA

↓ These Neoplan 424s run by the Saudi Arabian Public Transport Company (SAPTCO) were operating in Riyadh, Mecca and Jeddah in 1996. Photography in public places in the Kingdom is not recommended, but the opportunity to photograph this attractive minaret in Jeddah, timed to include SAPTCO **912**, could not be missed. The rear section of the lower deck of these vehicles is reserved for women passengers.

SINGAPORE

→ Singapore Bus Service (SBS) **7114**, a 1986 Leyland Olympian with Alexander body, passes over the attractive Anderson Bridge in April 1994. This bridge, a remnant of British Empire engineering, opened in 1910 and has also seen tram and trolleybus operation.

EAST 97
KODAK IS
Leyland
SBS 7114K

SINGAPORE

↑ This Northern Counties-bodied Leyland Olympian was built in 1988 for the short-lived Bexley Bus operation in Kent, and was sold to Singapore in 1991. In March 1992, it still carried the Bexley livery when operating as a shuttle bus on Singapore's popular Sentosa Island. The bus has since been rebuilt to open-top condition. ➔ All-over advertising can sometimes be novel, even artistic, but this is surely not a good example of the genre. SBS Superbus **9406**, a Volvo Olympian with Alexander body built in 1994, negotiates the junction of Nicoll Highway and Raffles Avenue in March 2000.

Only 1% Low Fat
High Calcium with
Vitamin
D for better
calcium absorption
daisy
HI-LO
High in what you need more.
Low in what you need less.
milk
SUPER BUS
AIR CON
BEDOK
14
CLEMENTI
AIRCON
VOLVO
SBS9406E

SOUTH AFRICA

↑ The beautiful jacaranda trees were just coming to the end of their wonderful seasonal display as Pretoria **290**, a 1988 MAN with Busaf body, was passing by in November 1998. → South African cities have always maintained the British tradition of the double-decker, ever since the days of the tram. This Daimler Fleetline of 1971 has a Busaf body and is thought to have been first used by the municipality of Port Elizabeth. By November 1998 it was earning a living as a tour bus for Elwierda in Cape Town and is seen at the lower station of the Table Mountain cable car.

ELWIERDA 021 418 5888
ELWIERDA 021 418 5888
CA 1576

SOUTH KOREA

↑ The dream of many Koreans is the eventual reunification of the North and South, separated since the 1950s. One of the most popular locations for viewing the communist North from the South is at the Unification Observatory located north of Seoul. In February 1995 this Daewoo BS105 was working a shuttle service from the huge car park to the Observatory entrance.

SPAIN

→ To many of "a certain age", a "typical" London bus is an RT, not a Routemaster. **RT1296** was offering a tourist shuttle near the Olympic Stadium in Barcelona in October 1991. To allow bridge clearance, the roofline has been slightly reduced.

Poble Espanyol
POBLE ESPANYOL
PLAÇA D'ESPANYA
CADA
½
HORA
SERVEI GRATUIT
FUJIFILM
Poble Espanyol
B 4565 FD
P

SWITZERLAND

↑ When this one was photographed in June 1971, normal-control Swiss Post buses seemed to be everywhere. Now they are highly collectable for preservation, being popular for private hire and wedding duties. This immaculate Berna (then part of the Saurer group) is seen outside Aigle railway station, waiting to take up duty to Corbeyrier. Note the right-hand drive, an aid to safer negotiation of mountain roads. → The Swiss company VMCV (Vevey-Montreux-Chillon-Villeneuve) is best known for its interurban trolleybus operation between these points. VMCV **37**, a smart but simple Berna, represents a bygone age as it connects with the local light railway (CEV) at Blonay to take passengers down the valley to connect with the lakeside trolleybus route at Clarens in June 1971.

BLONAY
CHAUSSURES
A L'ETOILE
VEVEY
BUS
VMCV
37
VD·745
Berna

SWITZERLAND

↑ This ex-Bristol Omnibus Lodekka (thought to be former fleet number 7165) had been transformed into a mobile newspaper office for the *Bündner Tagblatt* when seen at Davos in September 1992. Although obviously no longer available for passenger duties, it was good to see the immaculately modified vehicle being put to such good commercial use, in spite of the apparent lack of customers for its owners' corporate hospitality.

THAILAND

→ This BMTA (Bangkok) Mercedes has seen better days, and the overflowing street market doesn't make life easy for the driver trying to find his bus stop in August 1986. In spite of the title Bangkok Mass Transit Authority, the city has only in recent years invested huge sums of money in separate elevated and subway rail transit systems.

ปุ๋ย-ยาฆ่าแมลง
เครื่องมือ การเกษตร

THAILAND

➔ The magnificent Grand Palace complex in Bangkok makes an attractive backdrop for this pair of Daewoo buses in January 1995. The essential window ventilation offers passengers a degree of relief from the sticky heat, but ensures they are subjected to the choking fumes of Bangkok's infamous traffic.

USA

➔ An early entry into the low-floor bus scene were these Vetter/Minicars 7000Ds of 1982. Denver RTD **2510** gives free rides on the pedestrianised "Mallride" route along 16th Street in January 1994. To ensure safe kerbside operation in the narrow (non-guided) alignment, they were built with right-hand drive.

Glenarm
GOLDIE'S
Seating
compliments
of
GOLDIE'S
DELI

USA

↑ It's a long way from Shanklin! Another former Southern Vectis (513) Bristol Lodekka, this time being used as a Tourist Information booth in Denver, Colorado, in January 1994. → Gray Line Tours bought a batch of Leyland Olympians with Eastern Coach Works bodywork in 1986. **604** is seen at Fisherman's Wharf in San Francisco in September 1989, but has since moved to New York and is now in service as an open-top tour bus.

Franciscan
RESTAURANT
TAURANT
604
MUIR WOODS
604
GRAY LINE TOURS
Leyland

USA

↑ Before the days of mass car-ownership, many Americans visited their national parks by rail and bus. To cope with the increasing number of visitors arriving by train, the Yellowstone and Glacier National Parks ordered large fleets of specially built charabancs from the White Motor Company in 1936-9. Designated type 706 with an art-deco style body by Bender, these 25ft-long, 14-seat buses gained a reputation for comfort and ease of viewing (being open-topped on dry days). However, they soon got the nickname "Jammers" due to the double clutching gear change noises that echoed round the canyons. Most of the fleet of 98 Yellowstone buses were withdrawn by the mid-1960's; many went to private owners and some were sold on to the Skagway Streetcar Company in Alaska. Most of the original fleet of 35 Glacier buses continued in service until the late 1990s, or were sold into private ownership. In 2001 a major refit was conducted by Ford Motors to upgrade the Glacier fleet to modern standards, and similar efforts were being made to reintroduce the fleet back to Yellowstone. Glacier **82** takes tourists along the "Going-to-the-Sun" Highway in September 1982, as these buses had done for more than 40 years. After a major rebuild, it is to be hoped that they will continue to do so for many more years. → This Yellowstone liveried version is seen as a static exhibit at the former Union Pacific railroad station, West Yellowstone, in September 1989. This was one of the Gateway locations where generations of visitors would once arrive by train to be transferred to a fleet of Whites for a park tour.

2026

USA

This (probably) ex-Yellowstone 706 was, in 1982, owned or sponsored by a local supermarket (Van's IGA) and used for private hire and local heritage tours. It was photographed outside the Museum of the Rockies, Bozeman, Montana.